84-19

RHAPSODIES

& CO

FROM I

**84-19 Rhapsodies & Co from I**

by
Docteur Cybirdy

First published in paperback special edition, 2023
By Cybirdy Publishing Company
101 Camley Street, London NIC 4DU

Designed by Kaarin Wall & Docteur Cybirdy
Proofread by Afaf Shour
Printed by Hobbs the Printers Ltd

This book is typeset in Minion, Proxima Nova and Copperplate.
A CIP record for this book is available from the British Library

ISBN: 978-1-7396637-1-1

# 84-19

## RHAPSODIES

## & CO

## FROM I

Docteur CYBIRDY

**CYBIRDY**
Publishing Limited

"Science without conscience
is only ruin of the soul."

A simplified British translation of François Rabelais' wise,
French words, written a few years before 1553:

*« Mais parce que selon les dires du sage Salomon,
Sapience n'entre point en âme malveillante, et science sans
conscience n'est que ruine de l'âme, il te convient servir,
aimer et craindre Dieu, et en lui remettre toutes tes pensées et
tout ton espoir; et par une foi charitable, lui être fidèle,
en sorte que jamais tu ne t'en écartes par péché. »*

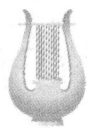

84-19 is a compilation of rhapsodies, notes, quotes and music I wrote and put together during the Covid era in London.

Over the past 30 years, I have worked as a medical doctor and adjusted, like all of us, to the exponential invasion of digital technology. In the background, another development was happening, unknown to everyone, post-genomic science.

Post-genomic science is the science based on DNA research and manipulation.

In 2020, Covid spread globally. Post-genomic science and digitalisation merged at all levels. A sudden disruption of human society happened, putting both human life and DNA in danger.

But why and how?

I was dumbfounded, even more so that I just could not see the medical signs of a deadly pandemic, a modern plague or even a kind of Spanish flu. Covid was not as dangerous as they said.

So, why this global orchestrated battle to save us?

An abstract tyranny was at play. From the start, the situation seemed to me like a dystopia with nonsense statements, misuse of numbers, no clear plans other than killing a virus and jabbing all human beings on planet Earth. Two wicked ideas, in my view.

I was in despair. So much misunderstanding, too much disinformation.

Post-genomic science was taking over the traditional way of medicine I had practised for so long. Society, as a whole, was in fear. Post-genomic science was disrupting medical care while digitalisation invaded further human intimacy.

Humanity was threatened in all its dimensions, tracked and traced. Everyone was dumbfounded, fearing both death and vicinity of others.

In looking for any possibility of human care, I kept doctoring and read anything I could about the new virus. I was trying to understand the new disease and to rely on apparent possible fast knowledge acquisition. However, distorted information was plenty. Without searching, I could detect not only confusing analysis but, worse, lies in the vastness of scientific information.

The so-called experts did not show any attention to details; rather, their reports were often wrong and always empty of morals and humanity. The few who questioned the science on the net got rapidly silenced on Twitter and Facebook, trolled and accused of conspiracy.

It was just insane. I felt my brain could not cope anymore.

As a survival mechanism, I switched off the news, stopped reading science and took refuge in literature, music and nostalgia. That has been my way to calm myself down and take some distance to comprehend what was unfolding.

I put words, melodies and images on the generalised bad feeling and despair with a strong desire to find hope and good vibes somewhere.

And magic happened. Truth revealed itself, and this very truth is contained in this humble book, a kind of cyber manuscript you now own and hold.

Nothing here has been influenced by AI or public opinion. It is the product of one I, a humble human being in quest of reality and hope for a new peaceful environment on Earth I propose to name Cyberworld.

At the time of Covid 19, George Orwell's *1984* and the fate of Winston and Julia under the watch of Big Brother came back to my mind. I read the book again and again while on YouTube, and then, words and meaning came to me.

In my reality and in the midst of my doctoring, musical memory popped up from my brain, instantly colliding and echoing with the Internet and YouTube at random to and fro. From the musical memories or YouTube or both, like the rappers of today, or even the rhapsodes of the ancient time, I stitched poetry, punch lines, metaphors, scientific questioning and music with a strong feeling of freedom and rebellion.

Dear reader, with 84-19, you are safe from infox and opinions of the know-it-all. This special edition has not been edited by any sensitivity readers. No AI, nudging, propaganda, or incitation either. No data collection in between. Just you and this very special eternal recyclable human memory receptacle, one unique book, an earthly object which is here to stay.

I did not write about masks and vaccines, no need to; everybody knows by now.

So, let it go. As and when you feel it, scroll down, turn it on, page by page, one or two, or three at a time, at your pace, your choice. Internet connection on or off, googling or not, your choice too! Smashing!

In your intimacy, alone with the book, pick up the thoughts, the knowledge and references, the experiences, the simple truth one other human being raw material is offering to share with you on your own time. Simply, humbly, feel alive and open your mind without any a priori.

This is crude human truth with sensual and emotional layers of complexity away from tyrannic rationality and hyperreality.

Just Enjoy and Think!!!!!!!!!!!!!!

discovered that gain of function's research has been exported and financed by the American government in Wuhan, China for several years. Gain of function is the use of genomic editing technology referred to as CRISPR (Clustered Regularly Interspaced Short Palindromic Repeats) with the objective of increasing transmissibility, virulence, immunogenicity or host tropism of viruses, in other words, to create a super virus for bio war.

Simply, CRISPR technology allows scientists to create a new virus, and that is what they did back in 2019.

**George Orwell wrote in *1984*:**

*Not merely the validity of experience, but the very existence of external reality was tacitly denied by their philosophy.*

Inspired by the YouTube video
**'Start the Healing' by Korn**
I wrote *My Desire*.

# My Desire

I have got, one desire
To see a new world order
On the aftermath of
The defeat of the medical despotism
And Psychosocial theory

My Desire
The cessation of Global Biopolitics
And of
The Medical use of Human Beings

My Desire
That life on Earth never to be GM
ever again

And labs
with Biotech inhumanity
To
simply and utterly
evaporate

On a solstice day
In a renewed Cyberworld
Of My Desire

# WHAT HAPPENED?

In 2020, the engineered virus spread fast. Doctors and politicians around the world were taken aback, and people died in the absence of known treatment in a disorganised healthcare system without any coherent international cooperation.

The UK realised the total dependence on Chinese production of medicine from Paracetamol to Rocuronium, the main pharmaceutical product to anaesthetise and intubate people in hospital ICUs.

Genomic research's role in the virus origin and the subsequent mass vaccination dogma, remained both overlooked.

**George Orwell wrote in *1984*:**

*"In the face of pain, there are no heroes…*

Inspired by the YouTube video

**'Bring Me to Life' by Evanescence**

I wrote *Julia and Winston, I love you*.

**Julia and Winston**
**I love you**


It was dawn
2020 Spring equinox
One of London ICU
Sick Building
with its deadly vibe
Chaos, MP 2.5 and a lab bug
Winston, in bed 1,
Julia, in bed 9

Winston got the bug and after 6 days on his sofa
A germ referred to as SARS Cov2,
A virus coming from a Sino-American lab
A genetically modified kind
Named
COVID 19
For easy people's grasp

Let me tell you
All along,
The so-called
Know-it-all
Will take us for granted
With naive words
And
Biopolitics

Anyway, on that very day
Julia got the bug too
Winston had it for the past 6 days
The huge man from the North got
breathing difficulties with
A bad cough, some shills and aches
Winston
Did not want to go to the hospital,
But when he could not stand no more
With blue lips and indigo nails
Eva called 6sick6

A few hours later
Winston
Arrived in HHC
Acronym for
Hell Health Care
Managed to jump upon like a gurney
Felt a strange feeling
A Netflix Death Row's souvenir
A scarry
Human impression
The digital hell
and
Big Data enterprise
will never collect

Let me tell you
All along,
The so-called
Know-it-all
will take us for granted
With their paternalistic manner
And their screwed data collection

Winston just could not breathe no more
The big guy got transferred to
ICU
Acronym for
Intensive Care Unit
Then
Tied to the machines
Many screens with graphs
Silent human screaming
Not disturbing in anyway
The unique sounds
Blip blip blip,
Blue, yellow, red lights
Vibrant buttons
Graphs, numbers
Digital hell dealing with approaching death
Brand new computerised respirators
Nurses and doctors not fully trained
Winston silently screaming, gasping for air

In no time
Through the translucid tube and
A flesh-piercing canula,
Rocuronium from China flowing
Reaching
The big man blood
In one single instant
Blockage of
All neuromuscular functions over his body

Winston, unconscious
Inertia to the core
Then
Intubation
A pipe in his huge throat
A black hole which has for years
Engulfed, let say
One tone of junk
Short canula placed in HHC
To be removed and replaced by
PICC in the world of
Acronymic communication

A nurse with tears in her eyes
And no PPE
Acronyms, junky words
Plasticky
Scary

A nurse
Assessing and waiting
For the VAT team
Craving for
Experienced human for reassurance

Tears now pouring
The MP2 mask wet and salty
The nurse just could not cope
When the VAT team
Took over
And skilfully inserted the PICC

Julia, 5 metres away
Still conscious
Smiling in spite of the impaired breathing
And the near-death
For

The woman has learnt over the years
To deal with
Shallow breathing
The beautiful human being
Managed to even smoke
In between

At least
She has learnt
Cigarettes and oxygen cylinders
Were compatible
After all

Julia ended up in ICU by mistake
Her vulnerability
Her BPCO, as they call it
Was terminal

The woman with blue eyes
Signed one week before the DNR
Meaning
Do Not Resuscitate

Dilemma in the ICU
Got Covid today
Should have not been transferred here
Or should she?

Inspiration, expiration
Blip, blip,
Blip
O2 at 90, BP at 86/66
The medical team around her,
Vitals worrying

Let me tell you
All along,
The know-it-all
will take people for granted
With their necropolitics
And form filling

The VAT came and in one instant
Without discussion
Come on,
We need to try to save this woman
Whatever
DNR ticked forms are

A skilled young doctor
Inserted the PICC and then
A bolus of Chinese Rocuronium
Instant comas
Intubation

48 hours of ventilation through the lungs
Of Julia and Winston
In and out, in and out
In and out, in and out
48 hours of monitoring
Injections

Nurses busy with split families
Zoom meeting prior death
To think of, pre-emptively
As per new Covid protocol
But when?

Let me tell you my truth
Right through
The know-it-all
will take people for granted
With their so-called
Digital solutions

Sadly
The unexpected happened
Oxygen pipeline pressure drops
At 19.19
Julia and Winston in cardiac arrest
Julia sensed the oxygen leaving her body
No return
And then,

Death and death
Death for ever
A sense of deep peace
Of escape
Final possibility

Julia, above the ICU crowd
Like flying
Soft, amazing lightness
Her attention immediately drawn by the huge guy
The caring team all around
Shouting, moving methodically

CPR
Electroshock
They all wanted Winston to live
To save the man
And use all their skills at once
And in concert.

Like they have learnt to do
Again and again
Like they are meant to do
As part of the human herd

But the inevitable happened
Winston left
All of them feeling like sheepish and exhausted
They will never know
What happened next

Death and Death
Death for ever
Winston ascended

And then
In front of his eyes
An amazing enlightened path
Wonderful, miraculous light
Mind-bogging and enticing
The Eternal light

The dead huge man from the North
felt an overwhelming sense of
Lightness and happiness

A woman in the distance
A beautiful being
Attractive
with blue eyes
Inviting him
To walk the Enlighted path

And then,
In the infinity
The couple joined in an explosion of light and peace
The light coming from the two entities
Embracing them for eternity
In the moral universe

Leaving
The distraught and exhausted team down below
In the HHC
In the
Hell Health Care

Believe me, dear reader
No sane alive human being gets used to death
Ever

Any human on Earth needs to make sense
To the whole thing
Even in the Hell Health Care
Each time, ever and ever again

The team tried to find clues
To make sense
To find reasons
They thought and decided
Winston was too young
It was unfair, unjustifiable
It was horrible

They should have been able to make his heart pumps again
All the team members were silent and thinking those things

But,
Family has to be called
And
Another patient was waiting for bed number 9
Need to get rid of the bodies
Swiftly, heroically
The corpse of Winston and Julia
were brought together in the mortuary
New Covid Guidelines were applied to the process
With efficiency

The young nurse with a salty mask died one month later
The trainee doctor who will be soon entitled Professor
got the virus too, but made it through

He carried on with enthusiasm and rage
His honourable work
To become in 2034
The head of the ICU unit
In a safer and cleaner hospital of the twenty-first century
In the new and moral Cyberworld

Julia's daughter will feel like deprived from
Her mother death
But will manage to reach Antigua in the midst of the
Covid crisis

Eva will be distraught, helpless and disheartened
when she receives the call
Winston had been a soldier in Afghanistan
Eva could not comprehend why she could not see his body
In peacetime and in the UK

Eva will do as she is told
She will isolate and just stay hours and hours on
Her Winston's sofa
Like hanging on to the
Multitude of photos of their past

Winston and Eva's only son, James
will go through bereavement with the help of
TikTok friends
And secretly will dream to become a spy

That is hard to tell
My friends
All along,
The know-it-all
took us all for granted
And this was the time of
An untold warfare of a new kind
A permanent war without a name

But
Truth shall prevail

In 2020, Luc Montagnier, virologist and co-discoverer of HIV in the eighties, alerted that SARS-COV-2 had a chimeric structure. He claimed that the amino acid sequence named Furin cleavage might be the result of genetic manipulation.

He swiftly got accused of conspiracy and silenced on the web and in France. A few months later, he sadly died, forgotten by his peers without any condolences from the scientific community and from France, his country.

In March 2020, in disregard of Luc Montagnier and others questioning, experts in charge of worldwide biopolitics alerted authorities and the Media about the risk of conspiracy. Other experts advised actions against human behaviour, and spread new words and terminology such as trials, shielding, isolation, support bubble, track and trace, shift of paradigm and welcome leap.

Despite antisocial words and measures, the virus of a new kind propagated all around the world and particularly in cities where particle pollution as the prevailing transmission route was simply ignored.

Nursing homes and hospitals remained highly infectious and deadly despite isolation. The virus carried on propagating despite mass vaccination. Both isolation and mass vaccination ended up being the most inhuman and just wrong solutions for the first ever genetically modified virus pandemic.

**George Orwell wrote in** *1984*:

*Later I shall send you a book from which you will learn the true nature of the society we live in, and the strategy by which we shall destroy it.*

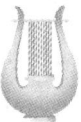

Inspired by the YouTube video
**'Counterfeit' by Limp Bizkit**
I wrote *Spooky spike*.

## Spooky spike

Hitchhiking spooky spike
Passing by
Specks of matter
And particles

Spooky spike now riding
The smallest of all
Named mp2.5

Spooky spike
Just loves fast riding
Fine air con, really nice
Whirling and whirling
Spooky spike entering

**I**

Speedy spooky spike
Through my lungs and up my nose
Pushed and glued
To my
Lungs lining

Glued to
My meninge layers
Sticking to my virgin lung

And
My innocent mind's barriers
Holding my ACE receptors
Spotting my lipid rafts

And then, and then
Penetration, invasion
Going through the various barriers
Nature has created
To protect

I

I, and
My own innate immunity
Just not fare

Does this Furin cleavage site of yours
Make you a GM creature?
Counterfeit and fake
Disrespectful
Of natural civility?

Will you provoke the cytokine storm
They all talk about?

Spooky spike
With your scary engineered domain
Are you the one
Who will kill

I?

The widespread use of mobile phone technology, social media, networking, and messaging enables a new domain of war, named by NATO, the sixth domain, human behaviour.

Cognitive warfare's sixth domain is human behaviour. Here, both the human mind and intimacy become the battlefield. The aim is to change not only what people think but how they think and act. Waged successfully, it shapes and influences individuals and communities.

**George Orwell wrote in *1984*:**

*Everything faded into mist. The past was erased, the erasure was forgotten, the lie became truth.*

Inspired by the YouTube video

**'One' by Metallica**

I wrote *Cognitive warfare*.

## Cognitive warfare

Warfare in the sixth domain
Amid
GAFAM treachery
Experts imbecility
Bad News all over

Covid
Came as a big surprise
The West weaker than ever
Scientists so wrong and hopeless
Spineless weaklings all around

People
Scared of a bug
Illusion of Free information
When one is
Nudged instantly,
Anywhere on the web
Lost in ubiquity
Tracked and traced
Without their knowing
Intimacy denied
Religion denied
Death denied

Trial fanatics all around
Life medicalised to a point of no return
Past medical care forgotten
All scared of a bug

When
Genetic experts rape
Human innate immunity
And animals' DNA

Corruption to the core
Neo Malthusianism
Poor Christianity
We had built cathedral on our pain
And now, yes just now
Guilty or victims, the only possibilities
Everywhere despair

The Western sixth domain
Endangered
Urgent Need of
Cognition
Courage and Volition
The pussies and the imbeciles will not make it
This is scary,
God help me

M atrix is a world of two realities: one everyday life, the other, what lies behind. The one which lies behind could be anything from an illusion to a dreamy world, but also an unknown and unidentified meta world of some kind.

**George Orwell wrote in *1984*:**

*Any sound that Winston made, above the level of a very low whisper, would be picked up by it: moreover, so long as he remained within the field of vision which the metal plaque commanded, he could be seen as well as heard. There was of course no way of knowing whether you were being watched at any given moment.*

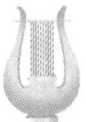

Inspired by the YouTube video
**'Last Resort' by Papa Roach**
I wrote *Matrix 19*.

## Matrix 19

Too much
Digitalisation
So much
Simulation

Avatar world
Labyrinthic
Matrix 19

Hyperreality
Modelling everything

Where is
Gentle Illusion
Within the
Avatar world
Of
Matrix 19

Poor humanity
Nudged in the UK
Policed in France
Parked in Australia
Woke and drugs in America
Woke and Drugs
Woke and Drugs

Woke and Fentanyl
Cocaine
Ecstasy
Hypersensitivity
Psychedelic
Matrix 19

Lab chimaera agony
Human despair
Hypersensitivity
Violence, brutality
God
What's our last resort?
Within
Matrix 19

Hyper-reality is a kaleidoscopic reality where physical and virtual worlds have merged. Simulation and the simulacrum blend reality and representation, with no indication of where the former stops and the latter begins.

**George Orwell wrote in *1984*:**

*It was a noise that set one's teeth on edge and bristled the hair at the back of one's neck. The Hate had started.*

Inspired by the

**Freddy Krueger nursery rhyme**

I wrote *Freddy Troll*.

# Freddy Troll

In our Hyperreality
Spooky and Noisy
Where is Freddy

In meta reality
For eternity

In our Meta Reality
Freddy,
Immaterial torso
For eternity

In our hyperreality
In the labyrinthic lie
Freddy Troll
Is watching you

In our mediocrity
Of our
Lewd
senseless hyperreality
will Freddy Troll strike
And How will he?

People did what they had been told and got used to being tracked and traced. They just reacted negatively when ghost alerts became too many. The system was then adapted, however, track and trace logic remained.

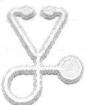

**George Orwell wrote in *1984*:**

*But at any rate they could plug in your wire whenever they wanted to. You had to live- did live, from habit that became instinct-in the assumption that every sound you made was overheard, and, except in darkness, every movement scrutinised.*

Inspired by the YouTube video
**'Freestyler' by Bomfunk MC's**
I wrote *Track and Trace*.

# Track and Trace

At the start the Koreans created an app
3 T
Track, Trace and Treat
The British as always,
oversimplified
And started Track and Trace
Track and Trace
Track and Trace
No treatment, just
Bimp, Bimp, Bimp
Track and Trace

Data collection
Surveillance
Care annihilation

From omission of one letter
The non-care prevailed
Despair and
Neo science destruction
Followed suit

Any assistance an author receives with writing a scientific article that is not acknowledged in the article is described as ghost-writing. Articles ghost-written by writers engaged by pharmaceutical companies who have a vested interest in the content have caused concern after scandals revealed misleading content.

Following the publication in May 2020 of the article "Hydroxychloroquine or Chloroquine with or without a macrolide for treatment of Covid 19", an article written with the help of ghost-writers, Lancet had no option but to retract the article. What was in it? Just lies and misinterpretations of data too obvious for anyone with medical skills not to see.

However, the only objective was achieved. Hydrochloroquine's reputation was off for good.

**George Orwell wrote in *1984*:**

*"…the thought is all we care about.*
*We do not merely destroy our enemies, we change them…"*

Inspired by the YouTube video

**'Ghostbusters official trailer'**

I wrote *Ghost Writer*.

## Ghost Writer

Lies based on true numbers
Who did this ignominy?
Ghost writer
Forgery, Treachery
Ghost writer
Acceleration thanks to
Ghost writer
Fast thinking
Ghost writer
Silly communication
Ghost writer
Hiding chimaera

Ghost writer

In 2020, Propaganda got referred to as Nudging and spread faster than creative and collaborative medical care, which, in turn, shrank like a skin of sorrows.

**George Orwell wrote in *1984*:**

*"His mind slid away into the labyrinthine world of doublethink."*

Inspired by the YouTube video

**'Freak on a Leash' by Korn**

I wrote *Scary staff*.

# Scary staff

Stay at home, Save lives, Save the NHS
No, never ever
I feared
It was insane
SSS
I read
Stay at home, Save lives, Save the NHS
No, never ever
STS
Stay at home, Take lives, Save the NHS
I hear
No, never ever
SSS STS
Lunacy
Stay at home, save life, save the NHS
Nooo

No more nudging
Please

Stop nudging
I'm so scared
It's insane

Western science is led by money and geopolitics and no longer by care, knowledge and ethics. Western science is global. Is this new science now controlling the present, past and future of our humanity?

**George Orwell wrote in *1984*:**

*"Who controls the past controls the future:*
*who controls the present, controls the past."*

*"In Oceania at the present day, Science, in the old sense, has almost ceases to exist. In Newspeak there is no word for 'Science'. The empirical method of thought, on which all the scientific achievements of the past were founded, is opposed to most fundamental principles of Ingsoc. And even technological progress only happens when its products can in some way be used for the diminution of human liberty."*

Inspired by the YouTube video
**'Did My Time' by Korn**
I wrote *Unnamed scourge*.

# Unnamed scourge

In the post-genomic era
Devilish ideology without a name
Weaved its way into
The Global power

In the mind of everyone
This was science
The saviour of the planet

It may have the appearance of
Popularised science with
The New English-speaking power
Together with
Rationality
And
Tonnes of money
But the scourge staid unidentified

Dear reader
I have found its name
It is not transhumanism
Or new atheism
It is more than that
It is worse
It is Neo science
Just like Neo Nazi
You know what I mean

Neo Science
Just like Neo Nazi
Insane rationality
And
Hate inspired by the
Feeling of a
Lost paradise

Obsessed
Turned on by the suffering
Of human being
Their plan
Name and shame
The new sinners

Conspirators
Anti-masks
Anti vacs
Vulnerables, the one
To troll and eliminate

French humiliation at the front
But

Neo science
Only interested by
Surveillance
Big Data
And our genes
Liars, Judas, too much PhD

Denial of history
And past experience
No cooperation
In their neo eyes
Genomic science
Must prevail

No chemistry or basic physics
AI, their priapic god
Phallic Big data
Human genes to manipulate
To rape and rob

Human behaviour
To classify
Record
To Nudge
And to annihilate
Their proposal
To save the planet
And to eliminate
our humanity

Transhumanism is the most dangerous ideology of today and is particularly active in laboratories. The very notion of care is ignored from the train of thought of transhumanists; that is what makes this new ideology so dangerous for humanity. Care and Ethics do not mean anything to them anymore.

**George Orwell wrote in *1984*:**

*"It was not easy. It needed great powers of reasoning and improvisation. The arithmetical problems raised, for instance, by such a statement as 'two and two make five' were beyond his intellectual grasp. It needed also an athleticism of mind, an ability at one moment to make the most delicate use of logic and at the next to be unconscious of the crudest logic errors. Stupidity was as necessary as intelligence, and as difficult to attain."*

Inspired by the You tube video of
**'The Bad Touch' by Bloodhound Gang**
I wrote *Transhumanism*.

# Transhumanism

Neo science
Paradigm in the mist of
Cancel culture
Transhumanism
Annihilation
Global corruption

Bioethic
Not ethical at all
Tyrannic
And
Dangerous
For Planet Earth
And its humanity

Neo science
Is boosting
Transhumanism Ideology
Stupidity
Danger

I n 2020 and 2021, more healthy individuals have been involved in research and trials than people severely ill with Covid.

During the pandemic, experts so loved and respected by us all have triggered without our knowing a disruption and a shift from medical care to research.

**George Orwell wrote in *1984*:**

*"He gazed up the enormous face. Forty years it had taken
him to learn what kind of smile was hidden beneath the
dark moustache. O cruel, needless misunderstanding!
O stubborn, self-willed exile from the loving breast!
Two gin-scented tears trickled down the sides of his nose.
But it was all right, everything was all right, the struggle
was finished. He had won the victory over himself.
He loved Big Brother."*

Inspired by the YouTube video
**'Come to me' (live in Cambridge) by Björk**
I wrote *500K Guinea pigs*.

# 500K Guinea pigs

500K Guinea pigs
In Albion
Clicking, reporting
Form filling
In the password inferno

500K Guinea pigs
Some only kids
Patriotic
Altruistic
Cash cows

500K Guinea pigs
Feeding big data hell
Venesection, injection
Swabbing all inside
No more intimacy

Jabbing
Questionnaire
In tempo
Jabbing, swabbing, questionnaire
In tempo
Jabbing
Questionnaire

Virtual torture
Ill-treatment, Torment
Care annihilation

500 K Guinea pigs
Victims of despair
What does it mean to be I
After all

Simple
Fuck it all, free yourself
Listen to Björk
with I
Come to us
We'll take care of you
And protect you

prescribed hydroxychloroquine for the first time in my life in 1991. I remember well. That was for a lady in great pain with Rheumatoid Arthritis. She got better and was grateful for hydroxychloroquine.

Since then, I have prescribed again and again hydroxychloroquine. No complication or negative feedback ever came back to me until 2020.

That year, trial experts used a toxic dosage of hydroxychloroquine, while some published false data and others simply used the old-fashioned treatment as a political argument.

Concomitantly, hydroxychloroquine disappeared from one day to another from the pharmacies in the UK to be back once the toxic trials and mediatisation achieved their fatal goal.

**George Orwell wrote in *1984*:**

*"The empirical method of thought, on which all the*
*scientific achievements of the past were founded,*
*is opposed to the most fundamental principles of Ingsoc.*
*And even technological progress only happens*
*when its products can in some way be used*
*for the diminution of human liberty."*

Inspired by the YouTube video
**'Just a Girl' by No Doubt**
I wrote *La coquina*.

## La coquina

Hydroxychloroquine,
La coquina
66 years of age,
Saved people from malaria
And alleviated human pain
In so many places

Hydroxychloroquine
La coquina
Trump got her
Like a little pussy
This could not be

Political correctness
From its pinnacle
Together with experts
Joined up and enraged

Without hesitation
With trials
They disqualified
Hydroxychloroquine
La coquine

They all
Misused and
Overdosed her,
Poor coquina
They

Censured and trolled your name
Raped and robbed
They
Hated you
Poor old coquine

Despite the empirical evidence
They denied the poor coquina
Of any right to cure
And be beautiful

Chloroquine
Hey coquina
Wake up
Come back to me
Despite it all
I will always care for you

Nocebo is the dark side of placebo. It is a negative effect of a medication which occurs as the result of a preliminary understanding or knowledge that the medication may cause harm.

Information and Medicine can both be toxic. But nobody cares and medical information, alongside agnotology, the culturally induced ignorance, have been developing together unchecked, making people at the same time sicker and more ignorant than ever.

**George Orwell wrote in *1984*:**

*"But if thought corrupts language,
language can also corrupt thought."*

Inspired by the YouTube video

**'Cold Cold Cold' by Cage the Elephant**

I wrote *Chorus of boo*.

# Chorus of boo

Nocebo, bobo booh
Pretention of knowing
Imbecility of the experts
Nocebo, I'm sick of it
Imbecile Mediatisation
Too much information
Oversimplification
Popularisation
Attention disorder

Nocebo, I'm sick of it
Transgenic mice
Gain of function
Vulnerability, yellow star 19

Nocebo, I'm sick of it
Tyrannic Bioethics
Blockhead Public health
Genetic therapy
Falsified scientist narrative
Lancet gate
Ghost writers
Media stupidity

Shielding, asymptomatic
DARPA-ARPA CRICK
Acronyms make me sick
Welcome leap
So wrong

Nocebo, c'est pas beau,
Bobo Booh
Just sick of it
Nocebo, bobo
Boo, boooooooo

I, a doctor, found only in 2020 and while googling that humanised mice were created and sold by millions on the web, not on the dark one but on the web any individual in the world can access.

A humanised mouse is a mouse engineered by DNA manipulation to carry functioning human genes, cells, tissues, and organs. It is a chimera, and it is cute, before scientists' usage of its body, obviously.

**George Orwell wrote in *1984*:**

*"They would have blown his brain to pieces before they could reclaim it. The heretical thought would be unpunished, unrepented, out of their reach for ever. They would have blown a hole in their own perfection. To die hating them, that was freedom."*

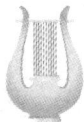

Inspired by the YouTube video
**'Basket Case' by Green Day**
I wrote *Piece of mind*.

# Piece of mind

19 of the month
I am in front of the screen
I can hear its scream
I moan
I groan
I cry and cry

Moans and groans
Piercing the flow of my tears
Still

I can hear its squeaking noise
The humanised mice
Scream
Blue murder

And in front of my screen
I feel
Hopeless, speechless without words
The only option
Copy paste
The only option
Copy paste
Copy paste
Copy paste
Copy paste

Google search for Humanized mice brain, on 19/10/21 6 300 000 results:

"The Jackson laboratory confidence in your studies. Humanized mouse model checkpoint.

Genetically modified models UCI develops humanized mice to study human brain cells.......chimeric mouse brain..... human mini brains make themselves at home in mice."

Humanised mice are considered by some a powerful tool for studying cancer, infectious diseases and neuroscience.

There are single, double and triple knock-in models on sale on the web. I feel for them, so I have created a nickname to address this chimeric being of a new kind, the Baby Micy.

**George Orwell wrote in *1984*:**

*"They were beneath suspicion. As the Party slogan put it, 'Proles and animals are free'."*

Inspired by the YouTube video

**'Tell Me Baby' by the Red Hot Chilli Peppers**

I wrote *Tell me Baby Micy*.

## Tell me Baby Micy

Baby Micy
Listen to the lyrics
*Tell me, what' s your story*
*Where you come from*
Transgenic,
Sweet furry trammy
I like you.
Have you got a name?
Listen to the lyrics

*Tell me baby, what' s your story*
*Where you come from*
*I like your*
Cute pinkie translucid
Sweety Auricles
Wet nose's tip
Snowy white fur
Let me tell you
Love your houppelande
Listen carefully
*You're so lovely, are you lonely?*
*Tell me baby, what's your story?*
*Did you give up the innocence they stole from you?*

In 2022, I got despaired when I realised that not only HIV, but also Covid and Monkey Pox are all likely to be the consequences of laboratory manipulation, and that, unknowingly, I took part in this scientific masquerade and cover-up for too many years.

**George Orwell wrote in *1984*:**

*"Nothing was your own except the few cubic centimetres inside your skull."*

Inspired by the YouTube video

**'Freestyler' by Bomfunk MC's**

I wrote HIV to *Monkey Pox*.

# HIV to Monkey Pox

HIV
From Congo
To
The World

Monkey's torture
Blood Vampire
Monkey Pox
Monkey to human
Lab manipulation
Monkey to human
Lab false transcendence

Monkey Pox in the seventieth
Came back
In 2021
Within
the Covid
Interstice

Liars and Scientists
have
No limit
And
No accountability

HIV
Covid
And Monkey Pox
Products of
Their
Stupid lies
And
Dangerosity

# HOW COME?

Today, some international experts and benefactors are convinced that we are too many on the planet. I have many times observed that the same people have got a visceral fascination with mass vaccination, destruction of viruses, isolation of non-experts and a love/hate connection with the human feral side.

**George Orwell wrote in *1984*:**

*"The Hate week"*

Inspired by the YouTube video

**'Last Caress' from the Misfits
and interpreted by Metallica**

I wrote *Hatred and Caress*.

## Hatred and Caress

They got something to say
They killed COVID today
And it does not matter much to them
As long as it's dead
Well, they got something to say
They raped my brain today
And it does not matter much to them
As long as it's spread
Sweet lovely death
They are waiting for my breath
Oh, sweet death, one last caress

Particle pollution may have been the main trigger for the rapid worldwide dissemination, amplification and propagation of Covid.

This very fact has been seldom noticed by experts in Global Warming, who have consistently failed to take a holistic view of humanity and its environment. They seem to me to be obsessed and blinded by carbon dioxide counting, human faults, reports and policy-making, taxes, regulations, regulations, regulations, ad vitam aeternam.

Furthermore, expertise without any sense of respect, as seen during the Covid era, can lead these very experts to dangerous stupidity and blindness to the big question: HOW?

**George Orwell wrote in *1984*:**

*"a feeling of weariness has overwhelmed him."*

Inspired by the YouTube video

**'Virus.Exe' by Drip Fed Empire**

I wrote *Strength without honour*.

## Strength without honour

Once upon a time
Wise scientists resolved the Ozone layer crisis
Why do most of them
now deny MP2.5 calamity?

Shadow on the past and
Darkening of our future
Illusion of things
Strength without honour

Neo scientists
Have lost the plot
And
Are destroying our immunity
Neo scientists
With strength
Without honour
Isolate us
from Planet Earth
And
From each other

My friend
Do not despair
Acknowledge
Recognise
And
Just now
Listen to Drip Fed Empire

*The devil is real and he sold us out*
*Cus I can see the look in their evil eyes*
*They drip-fed us on lies*

B inary thinking does not allow any accurate reflection of reality, let alone truth.

**George Orwell wrote in *1984*:**

*"It was as though their two minds had opened and the thoughts were flowing from one into the other through their eyes. 'I am with you', O'Brien seemed to be saying to him. 'I know precisely what you are feeling. I know all about your contempt, your hatred, your disgust. But don't worry, I am on your side!' And then the flash of intelligence was gone, and O'Brien's face was as inscrutable as everybody else's."*

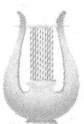

Inspired by the YouTube video
**'O Green World' by Gorillaz**
I wrote *Oh Binary world*.

## Oh Binary world

Do let me down
Make Silicon valley
Desert me now
Binary, just stupid

Binary tyranny
The lab bug got it
And adapted quicker
Than binary thinking

Oh, binary world
Do let us down
Dissolve
Return to sanity

Green mighty world
In my mind, Gorillaz melody

Chaos can be described as an exponential sensitivity to small perturbations. Chaos is everywhere in nature and has an essential role for all living forms. Humanity is both chaotic and sensitive to equilibrium because being human is natural, and the human's brain function is together chaotic and purposeful, that is why, human brain is amazing.

Current binary thinking of the experts not only cannot apprehend this very fact of human life, but also perpetuate the evil forces of humanity.

**George Orwell wrote in *1984*:**

*"Then everything was normal again,
and the old fear, the hatred and the bewilderment
came crowding back again."*

Inspired by the YouTube video

**'Great Movies Themes: Salò, or the 120 days of Sodom'
by Ennio Morricone**

I wrote **Natural Evil.**

# Natural Evil

Nature tendency to complexity
To both harmony and chaos
Nature, so ambiguous

Eternal Renewal
Adversity resolution
Both
In Nature's core

Natural mixed sex, Universality
Feral entity
Nature's way,
Diversity

Nature knows it well
Nature and Humanity
Similarity, contiguity

Sexuality and Love
Pasolini's terrifying truth
Anti-thesis
Part of
Sacred humanity

Carbon-free Human creativity
Impermanence, rebirth
Chaos
Reaction

We, human do know
After the shock
And against Evil
Common sense and Solidarity
Shall prevail

Because we are
Reactive Humanity
And we have got
Human ingenuity
And
Adaptability
Yes, we all IIIIII
Shall save
Natural humanity

For ever and ever
We shall be
Homo Sapiens

Our ancestral immunity
And our
Collective intelligence
Shall remain
To the end of time
With chaotic
human and beautiful
Truth
Towards a renewed equilibrium
And the defeat of Evil

In the Western world, the loss of social and ethical standards referred to as anomie spread steadily over the past 30 years or so. At the same time, medicalisation and denial of death invaded the train of thought.

Demarketing, with its gloomy and inhuman promotion of a healthy lifestyle. appeared and developed to settle into the fabric of the society. Life and Death of despair followed suit.

In the anomic alienated Western world, war on the sixth is possible as bloodless and senseless.

**George Orwell wrote in *1984*:**

*"He was alone. The past was dead,
the future was unimaginable."*

Inspired by the YouTube video

**'Keine Lust' by Rammstein**

I wrote *Denied Libido*.

## Denied Libido

So much cold
So cold, are we all cold?

Too much inhumanity

Once Hawkins and Elon inscribed
However,
Their open letter on AI
Kept unnoticed

Nobody cared
No one
warmed up to the challenge
Of Ethics and Respect

So much cold around
Is that despair
Or
Dehumanisation

They are all so cold

The post-modern western world is characterised by the desacralisation of humanity, sex consumerism, free speech, Nobel prized adulation, mediatisation of everything, and cretinism. But the worst and most dangerous characteristic of this state of affairs is transhumanism, a dogma affecting biologists and technicians. In my view, transhumanism beliefs has metamorphosed some of these experts into Frankenstein's offspring and money makers.

While Frankenstein inaugurated the Science fiction literature, today experts are sadly making science fiction real, inhuman and dystopic.

**George Orwell wrote in *1984*:**

*"The whole atmosphere of the huge blocks of flats,*
*the richness and spaciousness of everything,*
*the unfamiliar smells of good food and good tobacco."*

Inspired by the YouTube video

**'It's My Life' by No Doubt**

I wrote *Attempt of a hyper exclusive world*.

## Attempt of a
## hyper exclusive world

Suicidal & Chimeric
Genetic & Dolicocephalic
Systematic & Fanatic
Hypercatalectic & tectonic
Microbicide & Pedophilic
Transhumanist & Eugenic

Epstein, suicidal

New atheist
Ecocidic, I'm sick of it
Hush, hush
Epstein, suicidal

While climate change is again happening, the experts are blinded by Big Data and report writing. Big Data's violent giantism and meaningless numbers could lose it all.

**George Orwell wrote in *1984*:**

*"It was in the Park, on a vile, biting day in March, when the earth was like iron and all the grass seemed dead and there was not a bud anywhere except a few crocuses which had pushed themselves up to be dismembered by the wind."*

Inspired by the YouTube video
**'Big in Japan' by Guano Apes**
I wrote *Biggy*.

# Biggy

Biggy
Tyrannic genetic
Big data
NHS got
The biggest cloud
Of all
Servers and wires
Biggy

Biggy
BM gaties philanthropy
Bizosis rocket and Tesla bot
Apple Watch, my Gmail box

Biggy
Dixie fire
Pacific Garbage Patch
Slavery, migration
Violent giantism
French humiliation

Biggie
Cyberattack on NATO's sixth domain
COVID death and despair
My sadness

Biggy, biggy
My heart, your cock
Our human love
Biggy
Mesmerise me

From 2020, The Nudge unit, also referred to as BIT, advised the government tactics of 'deploying fear, shame and scapegoating' among us all.

**George Orwell wrote in *1984*:**

*"The scientist of today is either a mixture of psychologist and inquisitor, studying with extraordinary minuteness the meaning of facial expressions, gestures and tones of voice, and testing the truth-producing effects of drugs, shock therapy, hypnosis and physical torture; or he is a chemist, physicist or biologist concerned only with such branches of his special subject as are relevant to the taking of life."*

Inspired by the YouTube video
**'Human Behaviour' by Björk**
I wrote *Behavioural Insight Team*.

## Behavioural Insight Team

BIT,
Don't get the mickey
Behavioural Insight Team
Named by some Nudge unit
Nudging, advising
Propagandist, aren't you

BIT
Don't get the mickey
Your poison running through my brain
Your science will never be
My religion
Cause, no plastic ritual

BIT
Don't get the mickey
I shall join the swarm of us
Can't you see?
You're just evil instrument
You must disintegrate and disappear

BIT,
Behavioural Insight Team, is it?
No,
I say IBH
The Imbecile's Betrayal of our Humanity

WHO?

During Covid, I realised that genomic science, neuro and behavioural science, together with the novel gender medicine, were all based on bioethics, a concept misunderstood by too many. Bioethics is actually a vague concept, with an inappropriate and misconceived word.

So, I did some research.

The term Bioethics was created in the seventies to try to establish guidance on the ethical use of technology by medical science. This was never achieved, and both technology and Bioethics have been unethically applied to medical care in many circumstances. Bioethics experts never produced any code of conduct. Instead, Bioethics became a research subject, financed by Big Pharma with the only objective of regulating, reporting and labelling new research practices with no ethical feedback other than promoting illusive justice and gender theories.

Medical Ethics, on the other hand, is a code of conduct and is based on the Hippocratic oath. It has been so since the fifth century before Christ.

The Hippocratic oath, with its universal ethics, has never been considered by the proponents of the new branch of medicine, neuroscience, behavioural science, genomic and gender medicine. This may explain the consistent ethical failure of these novel branches of medicine.

**George Orwell wrote in *1984*:**

*"He was a lonely ghost uttering a truth
that nobody would ever hear.
But so long as he uttered it,
in some obscure way the continuity
was not broken."*

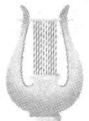

Inspired by the YouTube video

**'Ashes to Ashes' by Faith No More**

I wrote Hushers to Hushers.

# Hushers to hushers

Neo science
Bioethical
A new word from my brain
As I vocalise with Mike

*I want them to know, it's me*
*It's on my head*
*I'll point the finger at me*
*It's on my head*

Neo science
bioethical
Popularised digitalised pseudo-science
Only genetic, neuroscience,
Gender medicine
And global warming

Lies
Denial of empiric method
Or fundamentals

That is what I see
And
I chant with Mike
It's me
*Smiling with mouth of the ocean*
*And I will wave to you with the arms of the mountain*

Neo science
A word from my brain
It's me, the cyberpunk docteur
The 6th domain fighter
Genomic science
raped my brain
I, it's me

I am so
Scare for our genes
Cannot stand it
I want to name it
And keep chanting

*Smiling with mouth of the ocean*
*And I will wave to you with the arms of the mountain*

GAFAM, everybody knows Google, Apple, Facebook, Amazon and Microsoft.

**George Orwell wrote in *1984*:**

"*...the outline of your own life lost its sharpness.*"

Inspired by the YouTube video

**'Freestyler' by Bomfunk MC's**

I wrote *Al-Gafam*.

## AI-Gafam

Artificial
Intelligence
Google us up

Amazon control
Fakebook
Apple puke

Microslavery
Meta aversion

Whatever
Whenever

Make me five
AI-GAFAM
Humanity
Shall survive

In 2022, Bill Gates tweeted those words: "Tony, you were an amazing public servant long before Covid 19 struck — and now you are a hero to millions of people, including me."

Tony, as referred to by Bill Gates in this tweet, is Anthony Fauci, the current Chief Medical Advisor to the President of the United States. The man is a physician-scientist and immunologist and the director of the National Institute of Allergy and Infectious diseases. He is well known for his transhumanism beliefs.

He is married to a bioethicist nurse by the name of Christine Gradie. He is a good friend of Bill Gates and has been a sponsor of Peter Daszak and EchoHealth Alliance in China.

Following 9/11, Tony got promoted and was put in charge of global research sponsored by the American government. His mission was to develop American global research, genomic science, the development of Biodefence drugs, gain of function and vaccines. Tony, Bill Gate's hero, has, in a matter of fact, sponsored the gain of function genomic research, and as a consequence, the creation of Covid 19. He then led both the American response to the pandemic, and the global disinformation campaign which followed suit.

**George Orwell wrote in *1984*:**

*"O'Brien's manner became less severe. He resettled his spectacles thoughtfully, and took a pace or two up and down. When he spoke his voice was gentle and patient. He had the air of a doctor, a teacher, even a priest, anxious to explain and persuade rather than to punish."*

Inspired by the YouTube video
**'Le pere Ubu' by Dick Annegarn**
I wrote *Gaties, Fauxist and Ubu*.

## Gaties, Fauxist and Ubu

He has a tiny willy and a big ass,
Gaties Ubu
His madam was infamous and chubby dame
Melinda Ubu
Stupid and nasty,
The naughty pair loved only money
And Crème Mont Blanc
They had a plan for a vegan putsch
For a Pif Pouf Pan with a bazooka

He has a tiny willy and a big mouse
Fauxist Ubu
His madam was infamous and stupid dame
The naughty pair loved only money
And crème Mont Blanc
They had a plan for a rodent putsch
For a Pif Pouf Pan with a bazooka

And the day came when Gaties and Fauxist met
Twist Yayaya
Twist Yayaya
Etcetera

Following the meeting of the asses
Amid mighty flatulence, they all dissolved
To full disappearance
Only and sadly
In Dick and I's fantasy

Christine Gradie is Anthony Fauci's wife. She is a nurse and a bioethicist, in other words, someone pretending to study ethics without any moral code.

She got married, wrote a book, got a PhD and a directorship. In 2020, Christine was about to become the darling of the Media, a star of a new kind, a fake Angelina. She was interviewed by Vogue and told the world how, at the bedside of a sick man, she charmed her husband-to-be.

The Social Media mob was quick to react, stopping Christine's show for stardom.

**George Orwell wrote in *1984*:**

*"It was always the women, and above all the young ones, who were the most bigoted adherents of the Party, the swallowers of slogans, the amateur spies and nosers-out of unorthodoxy."*

Inspired by the YouTube video
**'No More Tears' by Ozzy Osbourne**
I wrote *Christinoo*.

# Christinoo

An imbecile nurse and bioethicist
Told Vogue, she makes her hubby drink a lot of water
She then said something even more puerile
Was about SM mob and the likes
Something like that
"It reduces my trust in humanity"

I say,
Humanity never trusted stupidity
And shall mistrust bioethics and its futility

I say, let us be pagans for once
Witness that nurse's cyber sacrifice
The bioethicist's dissolution
And
Full disappearance from planet Earth
Nothing less

And then, and then
In our Cyberworld
In our near future
And
our renewed Earth
No more Bioethics
No more death of despair
No more humanised rats

As part of the response to the Covid 19 pandemic, Jeremy Farrar, the head of Welcome Trust, has been a member of the UK Vaccine Taskforce and the Principles Group of the ACT-Accelerator hosted by the World Health Organization (WHO). Jeremy Farrar chairs the WHO R&D Blueprint Advisory Group.

As well as sharing his expertise, he champions rapid investment in research on Covid 19 testing, treatments and vaccines, and argues that everyone – not only people who live in rich countries – should benefit equally from the discoveries.

So much so that WHO, the World Health Organisation, named Jeremy as its chief scientist for its worldwide operations.

He is very rich too.

I say Boohoo and hatefully raised my middle finger to the champion of rapid investment.

**George Orwell wrote in *1984***

*"...but it is also necessary that he should be a credulous and ignorant fanatic whose prevailing moods are fear, hatred, adulation, and orgiastic triumph."*

Inspired by the YouTube video

**'Evidence' by Faith No More**

I wrote Farragor.

# Farragor

Once upon a time
Farragor wrote a book with a perverse title
And in doing so
Farragor fucked it all

Spike, The virus versus the people
He called it
Dangerous concept
In our DNage

The little devil
Just forgot the doctors
Medical science and knowledge

Farragor, you fucked it up
It was just a spike
A spooky spike
I know, I know
Spooky, spooky
With a GM furin domain

Farragor, listen to me
Darwin's tree of life
Now denied
Life is ENTANGLED

The Virus kingdom bigger than you can imagine
Genes travelling from species to species
I know

Neo scientists are playing with nature
And our genes
But you,
You just don't care

Farragor, listen to me
Germicide, we will never be
Farragor, little devil
Data fanatic
Wake up

The virus mutates
Quicker than your thinking
Virus life cannot be eradicated

In the post-genomic era
Your corrupted mind
Stupidity and lack of open-mindedness
Endangers Human innate immunity
You really fucked it up
Farragor, little devil
Of I

Peter Daszak is a zoologist and a good friend of Jeremy Farrar, Rita Colwell, and Anthony Fauci.

He is the founder of EcoHealth Alliance, the organisation which financed and organised gain of function research and the consequent creation of Covid19 in China.

He is known to be a champion in rapid investments and has been one of the main worldwide advisors for both Covid management and the dealing with conspiracy theories.

The man is a zoologist. He has never treated any sick human being in his entire life.

According to the web, he said once, "I'm a lizard guy". I still do not know what that actually means.

**George Orwell wrote in *1984*:**

*"...others search for new and deadlier gases, or for soluble poisons capable of being produced in such quantities as to destroy the vegetation of whole continents, or for breeds of disease germs immunized against all possible antibodies."*

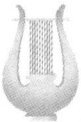

Inspired by the YouTube video

**'Unsainted' by Slipknot**

I wrote *From Daszaki and Zoology*.

# From Daszaki and Zoology

Words on the web from Daszaki,
EcoHealth Alliance, his agency

I read
*Who stands between you and against the next pandemic,*

Words on the web from Daszaki
Words from Daszaki and Zoology

I read on the web
*Working toward a world without pandemics,*
Indecency From Daszaki

I enrage while listening
Cory Todd singing
*You've killed the saint in me*
*How dare you martyr me*
*You've killed the saint in me*

And then, I read

*Why saving a forest in Malaysia has a lot to do with saving you?*

Lies, just lies, bitter lies
Lies on the web From Daszaki
Remind me SSS
Stay at home, Save live, Save the NHS

And
Corey Todd Taylor sings
*You've killed the saint in me*
*How dare you martyr me*
*You've killed the saint in me*

Daszaki web's content
Pure madness
See
One can read

*Why a healthy gorilla makes a healthy you?*

Inhumanity on the web
How dare?
Worldwide stupidity
From Daszaki

Daszaki, now listen to Slipknot and me

I didn't come this far to sink so low
I'm finally holding on to letting go

Francis Crick is a biomedical research institute and a registered charity. It promotes the manipulation of DNA and genomic science. It was established in 2010 and opened in 2016 with an annual budget of over £100 million. From its origin, the institute has close links with the Welcome Trust and Jeremy Farrar.

The institute was named after the famous Nobel Prize winner and eugenist Francis Crick, who, with the help of James Watson, stole in all impunity the discovery of DNA from Rosalind Franklin.

The institute's current leaders are proponents of the Paradigm shift theory and are all skilled at scientifically covering up the truth. Some are transhumanists, but all are very skilled at collecting money.

In 2017, the British organised a big party at the institute, referred to as the Crick 1000 meeting. Bill Gates appeared virtually to address the group of the 1000 most influential people in the UK.

As of today, CRICKS has not discovered anything worthwhile and tangible for our humanity.

**George Orwell wrote in *1984*:**

*"In the Two Minutes Hate, he could not help sharing in the general delirium, but this sub-human chanting of 'B-B!...B-B!' always filled him with horror."*

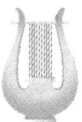

Inspired by the YouTube video

**'Sous le soleil exactement' by Anna Karina**

I wrote Crick, Crack, Crook, Crocs.

## Crick, crack, crook, crocs
## Sous le soleil exactement

Sous le Soleil exactement
Crick, crack, crook, crocs

Crick,
Watson denial
Rosalind robbed
Crick,
Gene dealer
And money maker

Crack cocaine, snowing blow
Crook, drug & gene dealer
Crocs letters on the sand

Crick, crack, crook, crocs
I call in despair
The mighty crow messengers
Huginn and Muninn

And the passer-by
Who has left behind
Crocs symbols on the Antigua sand
There, just there
Sous le soleil exactement
Under the sun, exactly

Acronymic communication and regulations are today the main tormentors of human intelligence.

Overuse of abbreviations and acronyms leads to miscommunication, mistakes and dehumanisation of medical care.

Since CQC has been operating with acronymic language away from medical ethics, there has been a concerning increase in treatment errors together with depression and suicide of doctors in the UK.

I also believe this new communication has paralysed in some way a sane reaction to the Covid 19 drama.

**George Orwell wrote in *1984*:**

*"Only the Thought Police mattered."*

Inspired by the YouTube video

**'Got the Life' by Korn**

I wrote *Charlie Quebec Charlie*.

# Charlie Quebec Charlie

Acronym, no meaning

C like
Charlie, I know
Calyx, that's nice
Care, no way
Chaos, possible

Acronym insanity

Q like,
Quebec of course
Quail, that's nice
Qualitation, sadly
Qfever, a possibility

Acronym stupidity

C, like
Charlie, I know
Core, that's nice
Caring, never
Coercion, always

CQC
May I suggest,
Chaos Qualitation Coercion
Or even better
Calice Quail Core

Bill Gates is omnipresent and omnipotent. Any politician on Earth is aware of his power over some experts and on global organisations such as WHO, WTO, NIH, Crick institute and the Welcome trust.

Everybody on Earth has heard of the guy.

Most know about his many passions, philanthropy, veganism, farming interest, mass vaccination together with prediction skills.

Indeed, the man predicted Covid 19 and is currently setting further plans for future pandemics, mass vaccination, mass veganism and more GM food.

Many are aware of his past relationship with Jeffrey Epstein, the recent death of his father and his multibillion divorce. Bill Gates cannot be referred to as a polymath, though. The man's failure at Harvard is known by some, and most of his diplomas are only honorary.

I do not know, though, if Bill Gates has registered his interest in cryopreservation. But whatever, our children will have to deal with his legacy.

**George Orwell wrote in *1984*:**

*"There are therefore two great problems which the Party is concerned to solve. One is how to discover, against its will, what another human being is thinking, and the other is how to kill several hundred million people in a few seconds without giving warning beforehand."*

Inspired by the YouTube video
**'The Devil in I' by Slipknot**
I wrote *The last colonialist.*

# The last colonialist

Spring Equinox 2034
Let me now
tell the story
the past, present and future
Of the last colonialist

Once upon a time, a young man
Quit Harvard and created Microslavery
The young man
Predicted the year before

1984

RIDLEY SCOTT APPLE FUTURE

In 2000, richer than a man has ever been
Much richer than Haiti
not so young but still creative
The last colonialist formed a
Foundation with hubris philanthropy

And then, Covidick unravelled

In 2034, we can say that in
2011, the richest man on Earth met Epstein to talk
philanthropy and science
We know that
the passionate discussion happened
Among beautiful white barbies
Victims of sexual conspiracy

Indeed,
The last colonialist made philanthropy
Its hobbyhorse, he will ride with cashy pride

And
Like Microslavery,
The man
Wanted at global level
Jabbing any human being on Earth

WWV

That was his dream, back in 2011
The barbies were amazed
But not enticed

In 2014
The man invaded British
Political correctness together with its New wave
Named
Popularised science
The man appeared virtually
At Crick 1000 party
In the institute opposite King's Cross
And
The snobbish British cathedral of neo science

Then, in 2015
The man talked at TED to announce
another clever prediction of his

## A PANDEMIC

Today, in 2034,
any English-speaking human being with common sense
understands that
The last colonialist expressed with verve
At
CRICK and TED
A wish for a new world order
We now call
Common Health

But in 2014 and 2015, among the glamour, richness,
technology
Political correctness
Science oversimplification and corruption
Denial of history, courage or even human love
Did anyone understand what was unfolding?
Did at least one of those guys know?

Today in 2034,
Nobody can answer
And most of the 1000 are saying
We did not know
Just
Like the doctors at Nuremberg in 1946
They did not know

They worked in good faith for science
That was all

In any case, it all happened
Among the total blindness
the last colonialist carried on
Riding globally his hobby horse with

In 2017, the creation of CEPI
Coalition for Epidemic Preparedness Innovations

OUAH!
Impressive
Effortlessly he corrupted minds of
Scientists
Finance sharks and bureaucrats
In concert with the misanthropists,
They all said

Let us all be philanthropists
Let us be the cleverest in the world
Listen to the master in innovation
Listen to
The guy who made most of us microslaves
Without our knowing

THEY CLAIMED

Let us be germicide
Build a worldwide biotech
And visit Epstein's barbies
Just be glamorous eugenics
Vegan or Nobel prized
Let the vulnerable die
And get out of this expensive healthcare for all

Let us be
Very rich and young for ever
Social distancing and masking
Work from Microslave home
Home, Home
Yes, that sounds good

THEN

In 2019, the worse came to the worse
Covid, Daszaki's invention escaped the lab
And
We all know
What happened next
2020, the last colonialist supported Fauxist
As proved by
The most cynical transhumanist's biggy mailbox
And with the help of
WHO below average human intelligence
Set up

COVAX

But, despite his verve
And his will to jab everyone on Earth

Covidick
The first ever cyber and biological battle
Defeated the West

The western sixth domain just lost it
And
That was
The end of the Empires
The United Nations and all global charities were vaporised
Western Pharmaceutical industry,
Corrupted to the core
Was found
Guilty of

NEGLECT
Of basic human care

Science publications
Corrupted to an unimaginable level got
Annihilated
To be reborn
All scientific papers to be written in
English, Spanish, Arabic and Mandarin
Ghost writers retrained
In translation and ethics

Medical care came back to individual care
Away from research
In respect of the Helsinki convention
British doctors retrained within a cooperative program
Involving India, Cuba and Senegal
Paris got liberated another time in history
And the French humiliation revealed to the world

COURAGE WAS BACK

The Digital industry was totally dismantled and reborn instantly in
A Global Cyberworld recognised by all nations
Genomic research deemed dangerous for the future of our humanity

HALTED

Humanised animals were adopted by the few Peta group members left
Neo science, its corruption and its lies all uncovered
Popularised science survived but
labelled as such in both Earthly and Cyberworld
False scientific pretention all the time tracked down

Nudging became
A sixth domain
War crime

Today
The last colonialist has been found guilty
Of PDS
Philanthropy Disorder Syndrome
His grand project of Common Health
And jabs for all or WWV
Unravelled and universally declared as
Ecocide, dystopic and inhuman

His supporters and Transhumanists have all been jailed
In their home and
According to the new isolation principles
Their right for cryopreservation taken away

For the future generation protection
Cryopreserved bodies
Have been jailed in their own facilities
Writers, spies and lawyers have been engaged
To publish a detailed and unbiased biography for all corpses
For it was deemed essential information
For the future generation

The last colonialist has been condemned to suffer
AS MUCH AS
Haiti people suffered for 220 years

The new world needed a strong symbol
To signify
The end of the Atlantic world
The end of the Empires
And its permanent war

It was time for reconciliation

HAITI
Having been the first country to free itself from slavery
And
Subsequently suffered from permanent insidious war
Haiti, The beautiful island
Became the main beneficiary of the last colonialist and of his ex
Gigantic money

With the condemnation of the Gaties,
The digital world disappeared
to be replaced by a Cyberworld

Soft and ethical boundaries
Between Earthly and Cyberworld were defined
Sovereignty and multilateralism both reborn
Together with
Diplomacy, the language for international communication

Multiplicity of Languages was defined as sacred
Human cultural and genetic backgrounds both described
as part of earthly sacred environment
Whatever the religion or the ecosystem

No more separation, no more classification
No more isolation

High human Intelligence with conscience prevailed

AI development was halted and redefined in respect of each
Human being
Data collection humanised
Biohazard, genetic or cognitive warfare all prohibited.

And

GATIES

Stripped from his fake medical diploma
was
condemned to isolate for ever
Without any computer
His essential needs got forcefully limited to
Hippocrates writing in both American English and Greek
One recycled pen and a notebook

Free weight
And vegan Burger
Until natural death

Gaties, the last colonialist
will remain in his home to be soon

FORGOTTEN

Dans les oubliettes
Tout simplement

Just like a long time ago
Toussaint Louverture
Fooled and jailed by one emperor
And French Humiliation

Cyberpunk is a word with several meanings. It is a genre of science fiction that features advanced science and technology in an urban, dystopian future.

Cyberpunk also refers to one unique Cryptopunk NFT, similar to the one that sold for 11.8 million dollars at Sotheby's in 2021.

A person can be referred to as a cyberpunk too. I consider myself to be one of them. I am rebellious, provocative and tech-literate with a distinct style questioning all justification of authority within the interactions between the web and the ground.

**George Orwell wrote in *1984*:**

*"It was not by making yourself heard but by staying sane that you carried on the human heritage."*

Inspired by the YouTube video

**'My Generation' by Limp Bizkit**

I wrote *Docteur and cyberpunk*.

## Docteur and cyberpunk

I have become a cyberpunk
Incorruptible and unstoppable
No more Armani dress
Chanel will never be for I
Cause,
I have become a cyberpunk

Newspeak, will never use
Be part of a brutal system
Will never be

Fuck BG and the imbeciles
F. the woke, I know my history
F. transhumanism, I know science
Neo science, scary
Neo Nazis and the like
Scary, all of them

I have become a cyberpunk
Cause I'm a rebel
Unstoppable Punk for life
Leather jacket, shaved skull
Enchained
Spikes in steel and silver
Piercing, my ritual

I have become a cyberpunk
Incorruptible, unstoppable
I Fuck your tyrannic empathy

I am a cyberpunk
One of the sixth domain fighter
You'll meet soon an army of I
Smarter than your phones

We are ready for the disruption
You have brought on
We shall fly and
fight for our humanity
And destroy binary stupidity

Destroy stupidity
On the Web for eternity
Cause, I'm a Cyberpunk

# WHAT NEEDS TO BE DONE

There will be an enquiry. However, this will not prevent another pandemic with a genetically modified virus unless laboratories are closing down.

It is possible the enquiry reveals the whole truth, however, and like before, most of the accountable people and institutions will not be bothered and will be able to carry on their life with all impunity.

Biopolitics, cognitive warfare and genomic medicine will carry on damaging the health of the population and its humanity unless this toxic global system is broken down.

In the post-colonial world of today, any human being is at the disposal of the westernised healthcare system and has no hope for independent health with no possibility of being listened to.

This must stop.

I propose the following:

- The clear annunciation of the end of the post-colonial era.

- Immediate secession of genomic research,

- The closing down of WHO and other international health and caritative institutions

- An enquiry

- The creation of a new system of accountability in global healthcare and digital industry.

As a human and a doctor, I feel close to the members of my species, to any human being on this planet. As a French intellectual, I know about the pain and history of Haiti, the first country in the world that fought slavery. In my view, the fate of the island exemplifies the current state of affairs and our future on Earth. Hence, I wrote *Alien culture*, inspired by both Haiti and our stellar future.

**George Orwell wrote in** *1984*:

*"Scattered about London there were just three other buildings of similar appearance and size. So completely did they dwarf the surrounding architecture that from the roof of Victory Mansions you could see all four of them simultaneously. They were the homes of the four Ministries between which the entire apparatus of government was divided. The Ministry of Truth, which concerned itself with news, entertainment, education, and the fine arts. The Ministry of Peace, which concerned itself with war. The Ministry of Love, which maintained law and order. And the Ministry of Plenty, which was responsible for economic affairs. Their names, in Newspeak: Minitrue, Minipax, Miniluv and Miniplenty."*

Inspired by the YouTube video
**'Alien Trailer Great'**
I wrote Alien culture.

# Alien culture

Negatively exotic
In the Atlantic world
Poor Haiti

Debt to the past enslavers
Blood vampire brought
doctors and AIDS

Orgiac Oxfamy
Followed suite

And then,
United Nation cholera
Got deadly
Cause
Rita Colwell
the woke and feminist
And her
malefic environmental theory

And now
In the aftermath of everything
Dogs of war
Gangsters of all kind
And
Welcome trust cash and pride
approaching
From the Cayman Islands

Gloomily
For the past 220 years,
Exactly
No one has listened to the excruciating pain
Of the islanders

Beware
Now
Is the time of the first war
On the sixth domain
And
One shall get prepared

In space and in the meta world,
no one can hear your scream

Human love has not only to be made, it has to be written about, again and again. Human love is first physical, but it is much more than that. Human love is together feminine and masculine; its intensity is beyond words and numbers. Human love is always caring and dignifying with respect at its core. It is beautiful, eternal, universal, infinite and is for all of us.

**George Orwell wrote in *1984*:**

*"He pulled her round so that they were breast to breast; her body seemed to melt into his. Wherever his hands moved it was all as yielding as water. Their mouths clung together; it was quite different from the hard kisses they had exchanged earlier. When they moved their faces apart again both of them sighed deeply. The bird took fright and fled with a clatter of wings."*

Inspired by the YouTube video of
**'2/5 Butch's bike scene' from**
**Butch Cassidy and the Sundance Kid**
I wrote *Love your ICYOU*.

# Love your ICYOU

Just love your ICYOU
My handy man
Cause together
Never bother of the lab bug
Cause together
Not scared of the digital hell

I love both your human hands and mammal heart
Feel your body through my core
And your words through my skull
Cause love you with intensity
And immensity

In our reality, no cybersecurity
No Gaties and no troll
No tyrannic genomic
No stupid acronym

Just love your intensive care
My handy punky man
661
Yes
Let us together
meet the Future

Whatever the battle, whatever the means of destruction, human beings shall remain powerfully beautiful, ingenious and creative.

**George Orwell wrote in *1984*:**

*"Tragedy, he perceived, belonged to the ancient time, to a time when there was still privacy, love, and friendship, and when the members of a family stood by one another without needing to know the reason."*

Inspired by the YouTube video

**'Weapon of Choice' by Fatboy Slim**

I wrote *Humanity, weapon of choice in the NATO sixth domain*.

# Humanity, weapon of choice
## in the NATO sixth domain

Invulnerable
Not genetic
Not resilient

Humanely natural
Invulnerable
Not Genetic
Adaptable

Homo Sapiens
Homo Sacer
at the mercy
of Biopolitics

But you Christopher
Beautiful Human being
You are
And will remain
The
Sixth domain
Weapon of choice

I and my family
Shall admire
You
On the screen

Beautiful
Strong and honourable

Yes, Christopher
you are
The
Sixth domain
Weapon of choice
Let admire
Again
What you can do
Christopher
The sixth domain warrior

Never ever before has science been so close to endangering humanity. Science, or rather neo-science, a new science derived from transhumanism has become the worst weapon the human species has ever conceived. Transhumanism has separated us to an unimaginable extent never ever seen before. Solidarity, intellectual honesty, human creativity and ingenuity remain the only lines of defence and are here to stay.

**George Orwell wrote in *1984*:**

*"You are a flaw in the pattern, Winston.*
*You are a stain that must be wiped out."*

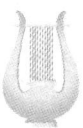

Inspired by the YouTube video
**'Bohemian Rhapsody' by Queen**
I wrote *Twisted Human Creativity*.

## Twisted Human Creativity

I say
A virus killed the artist
A bug spread by the blood vampire
Medicine and sex liberation

Clone looks preceded
Digital disruption

I say
The cyber post-genomic world
And its
Tyrannic neo science
Shall not silence the Bohemian rhapsody
And the revenge of Haiti

Both digitalisation and post-genomic science are using Big Data about everything one can think of. Big Data are images, Big numbers and genetic data. Averages are produced by artificial intelligence to make sense of it all. Results are not always mirroring the real world, though. The truth and its futilities are not taken into account. As a result, ignorance on the ground develops.

This is while genomic labs produce even more Big Data, feeding the experts' hubris and stupidity and their appetence for working on humanised animals.

With Big Data, we are creating more AI, ignorance and chimeric life.

The system is perverted but may not be to the point of no return.

It is now time to think and react quickly, don't you think?

**George Orwell wrote in *1984*:**

*"He fell asleep murmuring 'Sanity is not statistical,' with the feeling that this remark contained in it a profound wisdom."*

Inspired by the YouTube video

**'Californication' by the Red Hot Chili Peppers**

I wrote Nobody's average.

## Nobody's average

Nobody's average
And
Anthony Kiedis forever sings
*First born unicorn*

Big data, Graphs
All over the cyberspace
Number of cases
death or admissions

millions, billions, trillions
all over the Digital Hell
Number of jabs,
Injection, control
Big data collection
Siliconisation
Whatever

Nobody's average
And
*Anthony Kiedis forever sings*
*First born unicorn*
*Hardcore soft porn*
*Dream of Californication*

Big Data
Track and Trace
Daily publication
On and on

On and on
Numbers, just Digits
On and on
On and on
Denial of meaning
Whatever
Nobody's average

Poor human being
Digital industry
Collects everything
But
They know nothing
Respect nothing
Senseless Siliconisation
Insane Californication

But, and whatever
Nobody's average
And
*Anthony Kiedis will forever sing*
*First born unicorn*
*Hardcore soft porn*
*Dream of Californication*

Within the space-time dimension, at one unique point of time and at a determinate and specified location, my being is constituted of a multitude of links to my roots, my individual historical and cultural background, my immediate connections with my loved ones and with people around me. And within that environment and connections, I can breathe, see, feel, hear, smell, understand, protect and love. My hope for a better future is simultaneous to all these connections and sensations.

Therefore, within the space-time dimension, at one unique point of time and at a determinate specified location, my being is augmented by a multitude of connections to the past, present and future no AI can ever fully perceive. I shall ensure this and keep to myself my memories and my hopes.

**George Orwell wrote in *1984*:**

*"Every record has been destroyed or falsified, every book rewritten, every picture has been repainted, every statue and street and building has been renamed, every date has been altered. And the process is continuing day by day and minute by minute. History has stopped."*

Inspired by the YouTube video
**'Praise You' by Fatboy Slim**
I wrote *We've come a long way*.

# We've come a long way

I Listen to Fatboy Slim
And get personal
I think and connect
To who I know

Hippocrates,
Jesus Christ and Madeleine
La chanson de Roland
Les troubadours
Shakespeare and Rabelais
Beaudelaire
Hugo and Honore
Alexandre Dumas
The three mousquetaires
Jean Louis Pasteur
Sitting Bull
George Orwell
Scaramouche and the Queens
Christopher Walker
Fatboy Slim

All of you
I know you
And
I have to praise
And keep you to myself
Like I should

The timeline of Nudging, the new kind of propaganda, can be summarised with 5 dates.

Starting point: 2008 when Richard Thaler and Cass Sunstein published Nudge, Improving Decision about Health, Wealth and Happiness, the worldwide bestseller to be.

Then in 2010, inspired by the book, The Behavioural Insight Team was created with one purpose: to advise all UK organisations aiming to do good for people.

In 2015, Richard Thaler wrote "the purely economic man is indeed close to being a social moron."

Two years later, he got awarded a Nobel Prize.

In 2020, the Behavioural Insight Team, referred to as the Nudging Unit, infused at all levels the fear and inhuman campaign we shall all remember.

Nudging must stop.

**George Orwell wrote in *1984*:**

*"They would have blown his brain to pieces
before they could reclaim it. The heretical thought would be
unpunished, unrepented, out of their reach for ever.
They would have blown a hole in their own perfection.
To die hating them, that was freedom."*

Inspired by the YouTube video

**'Walk' by Pantera**

I wrote the ***Antinudging manifesto***.

## Antinudging manifesto

You nudge our behaviour
Is that so?
But, you can't nudge our DNA,
You nudge our stupidity,
But you can't nudge the great and curious

You nudge our behaviour,
Is that so?
But you can't nudge the bug
You nudge the system,
But you can't nudge the professionals,
You nudge doctors
Is that so?
But you can't nudge their ethics

The cyberworld is nudging you
Do you know?
Do you nudge its cybersecurity?

Anyway
You cannot nudge our reality

Can you nudge the woke?
But,
You can't nudge history and the universal
Can you nudge the vegans and the yoga freaks?

Anyway,
You can't nudge our common sense
You nudge political correctness,
Silly you
You can't nudge the lyrics

You nudge our religions and roots,
But you can't nudge our myths and rituals

So, listen,
Listen to me
just stop nudging,
Just stop human bashing
Just stop IT!!!!

Because
One single equation is the truth
(I times infinity) minus (phone+Mac+pad+pod+net)
equal US

Just stop nudging US all
Just stop nudging the collective
And…………..
Nudge and stop
The behaviour of
Gaties, Bezosis , Zuckery, Daszaky, Faucist and Kursweilet,
Transhumanism freaks and their lot
Vaccine makers
Stop them ALL
Stop their
Fake diploma, obscene phallic behaviour and rockets,
Money power, Botox face and RNA tech

Listen to us
If you now try to nudge our Kids
We shall proceed
To the sacrifice of your experts' stupidity
The bald or fat barbies,
Imbecile or despaired,
So listen,
For the sake of our Kids'
immunity and sanity
We are asking
Immediate cessation of collective nudging

All facts with a date before 2023 are true. Thereafter, it is the product of my imagination.

**George Orwell wrote in *1984*:**

*"His mother's memory tore at his heart because she had died loving him, when he was too young and selfish to love her in return, and because somehow, he did not remember how, she had sacrificed herself to a conception of loyalty that was private and unalterable. Such things, he saw, could not happen today. Today, there was fear, hatred and pain, but no dignity of emotion, no deep or complex sorrows. All this he seemed to see in the large eyes of his mother and his sister, looking up at him through the green water, hundreds of fathoms down and still sinking".*

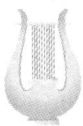

Inspired by the YouTube video
**'Zeit' by Rammstein,**
I wrote *11.01.*

# 11.01

11 January 2020
Announcement
First covid death

11 January 2022
In the News
First humanised pig heart to human transplant

11 January 2023
Possibility
Baby Winston 19 days of life

11 January 2034
Necessity
Neo science vaporised and stopped
Genomic chimaera production halted

11 January 2035
Hope
End of the Atlantic world
And
Of homo sacer

Renewal of homo sapiens
Peace on Earth and beyond
Freedom in a
Well defined
Human Cyberworld

That could be my Twitter status if I had one. I shall not write about vaccines either, it can only be too painful for too many.

So for now, I shall quote Francis Bacon.

> *"For rightly is truth called the daughter of times,*
> *not of authority."*

**George Orwell wrote in *1984*:**

*"To die hating them, that was freedom."*

As an aquatic being with Christian roots,
I shall hate them silently and trust the renewal power
of humanity on planet Earth. Connected to my deep
memories and the YouTube video

**'La Mer' by Charles Trenet**

I wrote just for you all, A child is born.

# A child is born

24 December
A baby's born

Not only she was the one
Who left behind
The crocs letters on Antigua beach

Marie became the mother
Of a boy she will name
Winston

A few months before
Marie made love in the mist of
The first battle on the sixth domain
He was strong and beautiful

Their unique embrace will never leave her memory
And will stay engraved into her core

The secret of humanity's renewal
Happened,
Just like that

One spermatozoon from the multitude made it
Marie's egg was in position
To receive the fittest and quickest
Which, in one instant
Penetrated the outer jelly coat
Of Marie's ovum

The spermatozoa plasma
Fused with the egg's membrane,
Decapitation
And then,

Natural Fertilisation
Mixture of genes
In the moral universe

And then,
The egg enriched by its genetic treasure
Travelled smoothly down the fallopian tube
To reach the womb

Where it will transform
Into a human baby
Marie will call Winston

She will tell him about Julia, his granny
She died
During the first sixth domain battle on Earth

Winston will befriend James
who lost his father from Covid too
The new Cyberworld friendship
will help the young boy to live without him

BUT,
At 18, Winston
will need to know about the man
and will end up in Haiti
planting Indigo Trees

Eternal Truth
Beauty and Wonder
Renewal
On our treasured Blue indigo Planet

To the end of time

This is the end of three years of human work. Three years of my life on Earth, I have, for you people from today and the future, written **84-19 Rhapsodies & Co from I**. That was my duty to our present and future for a better world for our children.

To finish off honourably, I have included in the following page the raw soundtrack and the official YouTube links I have been inspired by during my writing. These links have helped me survive and keep sane during the first sixth domain battle on Earth.

# SOUNDTRACK

# Love Your Book

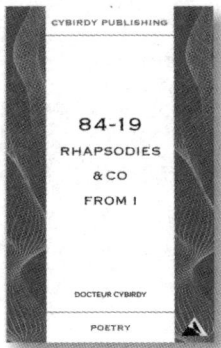

## 84-19 RHAPSODIES & CO FROM I

---

## TIMELINE

---

### JUNE 2023

*Soft-back book printed from paper that has been carbon offset through the World Land Trust Scheme.*

PRINTED by Hobbs the Printers Ltd
at Southampton, United Kingdom

PUBLISHED by Cybirdy Publishing
London, United Kingdom

**CYBIRDY**
Publishing Limited

## SPECIAL EDITION
Autographed by the Author

DOCTEUR CYBIRDY

### *Cherish your book*

| WHO are you? | WHO did you obtain the book from? | WHEN did you obtain the book |
|---|---|---|
| FIRST GUARDIAN | | |
| SECOND GUARDIAN | | |
| THIRD GUARDIAN | | |
| FOURTH GUARDIAN | | |
| FIFTH GUARDIAN | | |

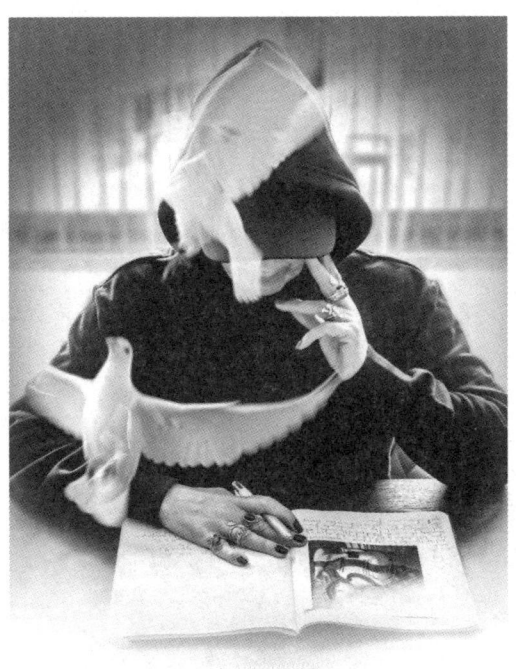

**Docteur Cybirdy** is the faceless author of *Hippocrates of London* and a General Physician. She has practiced medicine in France and in the UK over the past thirty years.

Docteur Cybirdy was one of the last independent doctors in the capital during the Covid era.

Passionate about ethics and art of medicine, she wrote out of despair, but with courage, *84-19, Rhapsodies & Co from I.*

# Other books by Docteur Cybirdy

**Hippocrates of London**

Published October 2022

In the pre-Covid London, a young blogger and anthropologist is sought out by the mysterious Dr Elpis. Despite the doctor's secrecy, Melo is intrigued by her open and honest desire to share her worldview in telling her medical stories.